# RESPECT

**B. F. MITCHELL**

RESPECT

Copyright © 2015 by B. F. Mitchell

All rights reserved. No part of this book may be reproduced or transmitted in any form or by any means without written permission from the author.

ISBN: 978-0-9963556-2-9

Printed in USA STLLC/Signs & Symbols Publishing

## Table of Contents

My Last Breath   6

Uniquely Me   8

Gone Too Soon   10

Manmade Hell   12

Warrior Queen   15

Mother   16

Love   13

Journey   20

Communication   22

Trapped   26

Blessed   27

Become   30

Failed Dreams   31

My Prayer    33

## My Last Breath

I will fight to my last breath

I was born to win and survive any battle before me

I am not a slave

Tensely receiving 40 lashes from the slave driver

-

I am a warrior

Losing is not my destiny

I will push on to victory

I will fight to my last breath

-

The eagle tried to clutch me with her claws

But like a lion I remain firm and brave

I will fight to my last breath

-

No challenge put before me can prevail

As I am a conqueror and wielder of the sword of truth

I am not one whose destiny is given to him

Or one whose sustenance comes from charity

I create my own way

And feed upon the bounty of the most high

I will fight to my last breath

-

Until my heart beats no more


Until this form of me passes away

And until my nostrils no longer take upon the air of this world

-

I will give all I possess

All that I know, and all that I am

And take upon the cloak of death only with victory in my grasp

I will fight until my last breath!

-

What a wonderful feeling to have

Peace of mind and serenity

Wow…you feel good simplicity!

## Uniquely Me

My birth was a miracle…
9 months, my beloved young mother carried me
There will never be another like me
My mind, my eyes, my heart
My ears, my hands, my hair, and my mouth
Are uniquely me

-

No one that came and is to come
Can walk and talk and move and think
Exactly like me
I am uniquely me

-

Inside me is a fire that burns
Which was ignited by my mother and father
No one can replicate my handwriting
No one can copy my swagger
No one can produce my offspring, B.J. and Cryssy
Because I'm uniquely me

-

My uniqueness can be compared to snowflakes
There are no two snowflakes that are alike
So I am uniquely me

**Gone too soon**

Eric Gardner, Sean Bell, Michael Brown

Tamir Rice, Trayvon Martin, Anthony Baez

Amadu Diallo, Marley Graham, Akai Gurley

John Crawford III, Jayson Torrado, and Mohammed Bach

-

A choke hold that snuffed the life out of a father who hustles cigarettes to feed his wife and kids

6 bullets to the body of an unarmed young boy who allegedly stole a pack of cigars

Killing his dreams to on day attend college

Many, many bullets to the body of an African immigrant whose wallet "looked like a gun"

Taking his American dreams to the afterlife, robbing his mother of a son

-

What is going on?

Blacks and Latinos are looked upon as criminals

Before they are given the opportunity to open their mouths

This belief is ingrained in the American society

This belief has seeped into institutions in the form of racial profiling

It poisons the judgment of those who are supposed to protect us

-

Latasha Harding, Patrick Desmond, Timothy Standbury, and Romaine Brismon

Gone too soon

This racial profiling will always punish and kill the innocent ones

For the past actions of those who look like them

-

It took 30 seconds for officers to determine that at 12 years old

Tamir Rice was a threat with his toy gun

Ask yourself how could society see this unfold on camera and not feel some kind of way?

This is clear that majority of the population believes the myth

That all blacks and Latinos are dangerous, even with a toy gun at 12 years old

-

Gone too soon

But not forgotten

## Manmade Hell

Manipulation of the brain physically restrained with bars and chains

Deprived prisoners of all social supports, complete isolation…group isolation

Cries and pleas fall on deaf ears

Punishment of a thousand years

Manmade hell

-

Do you know that prisoners are exposed to semi-starvation?

Exploitation of wounds, induced illness

Sleep deprivation, prolonged constraint

Prolonged interrogation?

Manmade hell

Prison

-

Weakening of mental and physical ability to resist

Segregation, degradation

Made to live in filth, infested surroundings

Personal hygiene prevented

Demeaning punishments, fabricated charges

Insults, taunts by the guards dressed in their uniform of police brutality

Manmade hell

Called Prison

-

Don't be a fool please

Stay in school

And learn the golden rule

## **Warrior Queen**

You, beloved warrior queen, who've arrived in my arms

It's as if you were lost from the start

My life seemed incomplete, powerless

Hopeless, forlorn

Gloomy and loveless

Till you came my way walking miracles in my life

-

Warrior queen

I had given up on love

You, beloved warrior queen, who've unlocked the gate of aspiration in me

With your love and compassion

-

You, beloved, must be an angel sent from above

To teach me divine love

You have led me to a place

## Mother

Without you, I couldn't go on

I couldn't carry this heavy load

Without you mother, I would have to be cruel, vicious, and deadly

Like they believe me to be

-

Without you mother, I would have to write swan songs

To my beautiful Crystal, and my beloved B.J.

Without you mother, everyday would be gloomy

-

Without you mother, there would be no need

To read, write, draw, educate myself, and exercise

There would be no point in anything

-

Without you mother, I am nothing

I am like the earth without water

I am like Jamaica without reggae music

I am like birds without wings

I am like a tree without roots

I am like Christ without Jah

-

Mother, time would not exist without you

I love you

## Love

I will not be engulfed with hatred in my heart for those who hate me

You distrust my speech, you belittle my style of clothing

You even follow me around in your department stores

As I inspect items I intend to purchase

But I will not be overcome with hatred because of your ignorance

-

You may even reject my race and deny me justice

Yet my love stands supreme

Melting the hearts of men like the sun softening clay

-

I love the darkness because it shows me the stars

So too will I applaud my enemies and make them my allies

I will build bridges instead of walls

With divine love

I will crush their evil intent

I love the light because it shows me what lurks in the dark

So too will I shine my love into the darkest of hearts

Until kindness becomes them

## Journey

My journey through this road is a must

If I want to be a better man

At the end of my journey a wonderful gift awaits me

I will get nothing at the beginning

Please do not tell me how many steps are needed

To get to the end of this road

-

I may encounter failure, heartache

Neglect and even lack of endurance

As I trod through this journey

But if I push on, I know that success is for sure at the end

Like Gideon Jah promised me

"Surely, I will be with you."

-

I will not make excuses nor put limitations on myself

Always will I trod another mile

If that isn't enough, I will walk yet another

Nothing can cause me to give up, no matter the heavy rain

And the unbearable heat

I will persist until I'm at the end of my journey

-

I will ignore all obstacles at my feet and keep my eyes on the prize

For I know that at the end of this journey

A wonderful gift awaits


Wrapped by his majesty

## Communication

Think it, then say it, and manifest it

Once spoken it becomes the first stage of communication

Never trap it or repress it, but always express it

Communication is a must…

-

If founded in the truth, then you should discuss it

Just like in God we trust!

Facial expressions and hand movements you'll even find

Communication through body movements

-

Shifty eyes, wicked grins

Cross your T's and dot your I's

Listen to the words that are not being said

Then read between the lines and you'll comprehend

-

Telepathic communication is how Rastas passed information

All happening since creation

My granny communicated to me in a vision

Telling me to stay away from the trigger happy ones who lacked communication skills

When communication comes, you better know

How to read between the lines and free your mind

It may spare your life

-

From our mind's frontal cortex comes the power of telekinesis

Once upon a time our ancestors mastered moving objects

They built bridges with granite, ten tons of blocks with incision

Done with communicated precision

-

Communication from Ra that the Egyptians comprehended

Then out of the sands came the pyramids

Lack of communication isn't a joke

This is the reason many relationships go up in smoke…puff

-

My lady tried to communicate to me "don't play the field"

But lack of communication led me to wheel and deal

She was having a premonition, communication trying to save our relation

Ship sink by loose lips

I thought my lady was a trip

-

Human relations to world exploitations

From the greed of men comes our damnation

Missing communication, you have one world leader ready

To turn the switch all because another world leader

Keeps on running his lips

A misunderstanding because of lack of communication

And with bad judgments bombs start to fly!

## Trapped

Forced to hear these noises in my head

No volume control

No mute button to tune out the everyday, hurting sound

Trapped in this unorthodox box made of steel

-

Turn keys, many of whom have no concept of what real power is

And never will

So whatever power they secure

They abuse at will

-

Could it be because I'm trapped in this unorthodox box made of steel

Why you fix your mouth to bark

Quasi tough!

You disrespect my family when they visit

You dump my mail in the trash and you refuse to talk to my kind with respect

-

Could it be because I'm trapped in this unorthodox box

Why you pretend to be super man

**Blessed**

Blessed with your black skin

Destined to win

Try your best

To stay away from sin

Your power and your divine might

Comes from within

-

Traps set in the journey of life

Forced to play your hand

With the cards you're dealt

Many lost track

Because they only sought wealth

-

Tap into your soul

And find the power of your black skin

Destined to win

Do not settle for the status quo

You can be greater than an athlete or an entertainer

-

How about becoming a judge, a lawyer

A doctor, scientist

Teacher, or even a lawmaker?

Do not falter or drop the ball

But work harder than the generations of past

And be confident with your black skin

That you are destined to win

-

Do not be like a tree without roots

Check all the ruins of palaces and royal tombs in Africa

And you will get a glimpse

Of the grandeur, power, and wealth

That your ancestors possessed

Surely you will see that

You are blessed with your black skin

Destined to win

-

To know yourself

Is to love yourself

Your ancestors were the first to domesticate

The cow, goat, and sheep

The trial by jury concept

Was developed by your ancestors

Be proud and know that

You are blessed with your black skin

And destined to win

## Become

My incarceration will become my redemption

My loneliness will become my motivation

My pain will become my strength

-

My tears will become my energy

My sickness will become my testimony

My error of judgment will become my lesson

-

My hate will become my humility

My life, my journey, my destiny

**Failed Dreams**

Faded Dreams

Twisted schemes

Triple beams

Trigga happy teams

-

Boys in blue

Alphabet crew

Comin' for you

-

Ballistics tested

Bail lifted

Prosecutors lied to see you fry

Lawyers tried to save your life

-

State of mind

Delirium

Max or medium?

-

Is it a dream?

No, just faded dreams

Twisted schemes

Triple beams

And trigga happy teams

Wake up youngsters

## My Prayer

O blessed creator, help me to see evil when it is around me

Increase the vibration of my mental and spiritual consciousness

So that I will never be tricked by the devil

-

O blessed most high, I ask that you influence my speech and my behavior

So that my words will never be used as a weapon or tool to hurt anyone

But to uplift and be used as a tool of construction

-

O blessed supreme one, help me to recognize good people when they are around me

So that I will show kindness and return goodness unto them

O blessed Jah, thank you for your love, mercy, and forgiveness

www.ingramcontent.com/pod-product-compliance
Lightning Source LLC
Chambersburg PA
CBHW032115040426
42337CB00040B/705